A Nest of Wood Ducks

by Evelyn Shaw

Pictures by Cherryl Pape

A Science I CAN READ Book

HARPER & ROW, PUBLISHERS
New York, Hagerstown, San Francisco, London

Library of Congress Cataloging in Publication Data

Shaw, Evelyn S.

  A nest of wood ducks.

  (A Science I can read book)
  SUMMARY: Chronicles the first year of life for
a brood of wood ducklings.
    1. Wood duck—Juvenile literature. [1. Ducks]
I. Pape, Cherryl. II. Title.
QL696.A52S5 1976 598.4'1 76-3833
ISBN 0-06-025591-9
ISBN 0-06-025592-7 lib. bdg.

To Freddy

It is spring
in the forest.
Young green leaves
are on the trees.
Small birds
sing their spring songs.

5

On a little lake

two fat birds

swim side by side.

They are wood ducks.

The male wood duck

is called a drake.

He has bright feathers

that shine in the sun.

The female wood duck
is called a hen.

Her feathers do not shine.

These wood ducks are mates.

The hen has a nest

near the lake.

She swims away from the drake.

She flaps her wings

and flies up to a tree.

There is a small hole
in the trunk of the tree.
The hen squeezes
her fat body
through the hole.

Inside

it is dark and quiet.

Her nest is here.

The nest is made of her feathers

and bits of leaves.

Six eggs

are in the nest.

The hen has laid
one egg each day
for six days.
Today she lays
another egg.
Then she wiggles
her fat body
around the nest.
She is covering the eggs
with the feathers and leaves.
They are hidden now,
from snakes and other animals.

The hen goes

out of the tree.

The drake is waiting for her.

They fly around.

They look for

seeds, acorns,

berries, and weeds.

They drink water.

They clean and fluff

their feathers.

At night,

the hen and drake rest together

on a tree branch.

14

Early the next morning

the hen flies

to her tree nest.

She squeezes another egg

out of her body.

Then she plucks
soft feathers
from her chest.
She puts these feathers
into her nest.

Now the hen will stay in the nest.

For about thirty days

she will sit on the eggs.

This will keep them warm.

The leaves and feathers

will keep them warm, too.

Inside the eggs

baby ducks

will begin to grow.

The hen sits on her eggs

most of the day

and all of the night.

The hen goes out

for a short time

in the morning

and in the evening.

The drake

is always waiting for her.

They fly around together.

They eat and drink

and clean their feathers.

Then both birds

fly back to the tree.

The hen goes in.

The drake stays out.

He will wait

until she comes out again.

Days pass by.

A baby duck is growing

inside each egg.

Its food is the egg yolk.

The yolk is the yellow part

of the egg.

After thirty days

the yolks are gone.

The ducklings

are big enough to hatch.

They can twist and turn

inside the eggs.

One duckling begins

to crack open

its shell.

This is called pipping.

Another duckling

pips its shell,

and another, and another.

Hours later

all the ducklings hatch.

They are wet and sticky.

They hop around
near their mother.
She will keep sitting
in the nest
until their feathers
are dry.
The hen makes soft sounds.
Suddenly she stops.

There is a noise
at the nest hole.

A squirrel puts his head

into the hole.

The tree hole was once his home.

But it is the hen's home now.

She will not let him

come in.

The next day

the ducklings are dry.

Their feathers are

soft and fluffy.

Plee. Plee. Plee.

The ducklings call to each other

and jump up and down.

They are ready

to leave the nest.

They are ready

to swim and find food.

The hen looks out of the hole.

She does not see

any animals.

It is safe to go out.

The hen jumps into the lake.

Kuk, kuk, kuk, kuk, kuk.

She is calling the ducklings.

Inside the tree nest
the ducklings hear her.
They hop up and down.
One duckling climbs
up to the top of the hole.
The duckling uses its claws
to climb.

The duckling looks out.

Then it spreads its wings
and floats
down onto the water.

The duckling swims

to its mother.

Then another duckling

floats down,

and another, and another.

Each one swims to the hen.

Now six ducklings are with the hen.

She is getting ready

to swim away with them.

But she stops.

There are sounds

coming from the nest.

Two ducklings are still inside.

They are not as strong

as the others.

They try to climb

up to the top of the hole,

but they fall down.

Finally

one duckling gets to the top.

The other duckling does, too.

They jump out

and swim to the hen.

The hen listens
for more sounds from the nest
but she does not hear any.
Then she swims away
with the eight ducklings
close to her.

Now the hen and ducklings
will live on the lake.

The drake flew away

before the ducklings hatched.

The hen must take care of

the ducklings by herself.

Many animals like to eat ducklings.

The hen watches for these animals.

She listens for strange noises.

The family swims near
some water plants.
A snapping turtle
is hiding inside the plants.
The hen does not know it.

The turtle moves closer.

The hen hears him.

She makes a warning sound.

She swims fast.

The ducklings swim fast.

But one duckling

does not swim fast enough.

The snapping turtle

opens its mouth.

It eats the duckling.

The next morning,

a big fish

sees the duckling family.

It swims up

and sucks a duckling

into its mouth.

48

Only six ducklings are left.

For about two months

they stay close to their mother.

They listen to her calls.

They follow her

wherever she goes.

They chase
dragonflies,
grasshoppers,
and mosquitoes.

At first

the ducklings do not get them.

They try again and again.

Finally, they are

fast enough to catch them.

The ducklings also eat seeds.

The ducklings try to hide

from animals that may eat them.

On the lake

they dive under the water.

On land

they sit close to the ground

and do not move.

Days pass by.

The ducklings are growing bigger.

They lose their baby feathers

and grow flying feathers.

Now they do not need

the hen to take care of them.

They can fly.

Soon they join

other wood ducks

and fly away

for the winter.

So does the hen.

The next spring

a young hen flies to the lake.

A drake is with her.

They are mates.

The hen is looking for a nest.

She looks into holes in the trees.

One hole

belongs to woodpeckers.

Another hole belongs to a squirrel.

Another hole is empty,

but she does not take that one.

The young hen

goes into one more hole.

Inside

it is dark and quiet.

There are feathers

and bits of leaves in the hole.

It is an old nest,

made by another hen.

The young hen

chooses this place

to lay her eggs.

It·is a special place,

but the hen does not know it.

It is the nest

where she hatched

last summer.

AUTHOR'S NOTE

The scientific name of the wood duck is *Aix sponsa*.

Wood ducks are found in North America. They live in open woodlands around lakes and along streams.

DATE DUE